MANIFEST

Your

Dreams

Renée McRae

Other Titles by Renée McRae:

Truth In Rhyme
ISBN# 0-9670542-0-6

Stepping Stones to Success
ISBN # 9781600135002

Mastering the Art of Success
ISBN # 979-1-60013-996-3

Night, Night, Sleep-Write
ISBN # 978-0-9670542-7-8

Keeping Your Cool
ISBN # 978-0-9990930-7-8

MANIFEST YOUR DREAMS

Create Your Life With
Poetic Affirmations

Written by Renée McRae
Copyright © 2022 by Renée McRae
Published by Poetic Motivations LLC

www.poeticmotivations.com

Cover Design by Renée McRae
ISBN: 979-8-9858379-0-2

Dedicated to My Grandmother:

Lucy Marie Burns
2/22/1915 – 2/22/1974

Publication Date
2/22/22

"Remember, on the Road to Success there are no benches."

Lucy Marie Burns

Special Thank You To:

My Daughters, **Sumayah & June**, for your constant support and encouragement

My Husband, **Jeff**, who is always there for me anticipating every need before I need it

My Mom, **June Bunch**, who has always supported me at every turn and in every venture!

(Inside Joke: "What's Renée doing now?")

And last, but certainly not least,

My Baby Granddaughter, **Teriyah**, who has put a twinkle in my eye, expanded my heart, and shone a new light into my life.

With Love & Gratitude:

Ananda Abinou

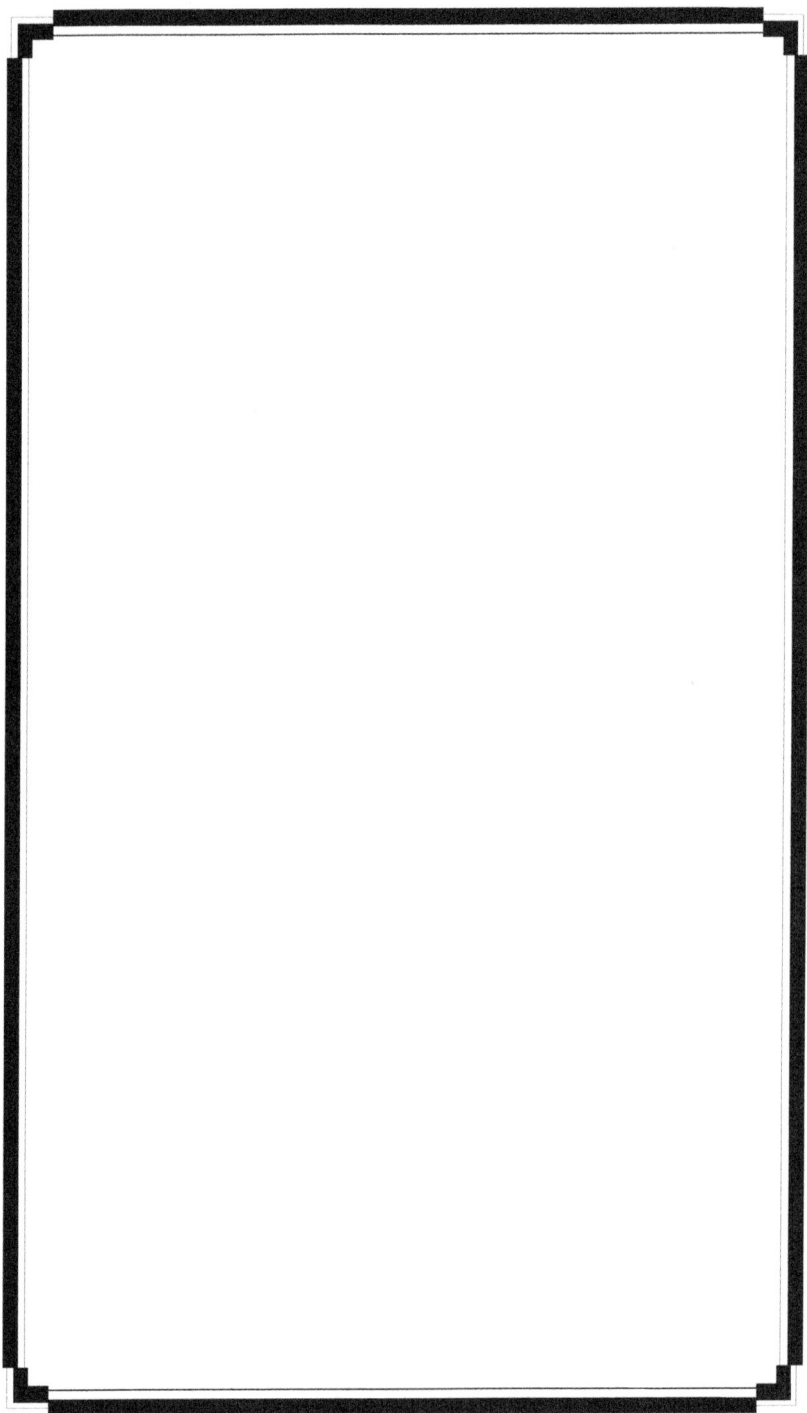

FORWARD
By Relentless Aaron

In all the history of the world, poets resound, they relate and they resolve. From William Shakespeare to Maya Angelou; from 2Pac Shakur to Alicia Keys; we've heard the poems, they've affected our walk, and we keep them tucked in our minds during our life's journey. Renée McRae, in her latest book of poems, more surgically connects with our souls in a way no other poet can, and in ways that her past script cannot. See, Renée's consciousness, experience and her spirit are forces that have already warmed us in poems like Give Me A Break and (My favorite) I Have The Power. But this is an evolved Author who has weathered her own life's storms. She's overcome her own battles, and it only makes sense to bring it forward: the teaching, the talent and the testimony. If you haven't already embraced her voice, her mind and her "power," then let me be the first to introduce to you... and re-introduce to others, my friend, the profound and gifted, Renée McRae, and her new work of art and inspiration: **Manifest Your Dreams**.

How to Use this Book

1)   With your eyes closed, hold this book in your hands and a question in your mind. Fan through the pages and stop at a page when you feel it is the right time. That page contains your answer; OR

2)   Starting with Page 1, every day focus on a new Rhyming Affirmation or Quote for the day or the week; OR

3)   Each day leaf through the book and randomly choose a Rhyming Affirmation or Quote that you feel is right for you or "calling you," and focus on that one for the day or the week.

ALSO, there are journal pages provided conveniently next to each Rhyming Affirmation or Quote for you to create notes about any of your personal meanings or goals. Additionally, you can rewrite the text making it more personal and powerful for you to achieve your desired outcome.

Message To The Reader

Congratulations! I am so excited you have chosen to commit to your path of conscious creation through the use of affirmations! Affirmations have long been used as a gentle reminder, or an aggressive strategy, in the quest to deliberately and consciously manifest one's life.

I've chosen to write and share these positive poetic affirmations and quotes in an effort to assist you in creating the life you truly desire, (sooner rather than later). As you already know, words matter, literally. Matter - as in materialize. So, mind your words as you would your manners, and you shall have the life of your dreams.

All my best to you as you stay ever so vigilant in remaining aware of your thoughts, words & beliefs, and continue to create the life you richly deserve and were born to live!

Renée McRae

Thoughts & Notes:

What is your purpose?
Why'd you show up on this earth?
What do you want to achieve?
What's the reason for your birth?

Thoughts & Notes:

_____

_____

_____

_____

_____

_____

_____

_____

_____

_____

_____

_____

_____

_____

_____

_____

_____

_____

_____

_____

_____

With the thoughts I think
And the words I say
I'm creating my life
Every day

Thoughts & Notes:

_____

_____

_____

_____

_____

_____

_____

_____

_____

_____

_____

_____

_____

_____

_____

_____

_____

_____

_____

"What are you afraid of
Why do you live a lie?

Don't you know the world is yours
And it's time for you to fly?"

The Universe

Thoughts & Notes:

_____
_____
_____
_____
_____
_____
_____
_____
_____
_____
_____
_____
_____
_____
_____
_____
_____
_____
_____
_____

This is a Boomerang Universe

I am Love

I Speak Love

I Give Love

And all that comes back to me

Is Love

Thoughts & Notes:

_____

_____

_____

_____

_____

_____

_____

_____

_____

_____

_____

_____

_____

_____

_____

_____

_____

_____

_____

_____

_____

We tell the story
And then
We live the story

Thoughts & Notes:

I'm learning, I'm growing
I'm beginning to flower
I now realize
I have the Power!

Thoughts & Notes:

_____

_____

_____

_____

_____

_____

_____

_____

_____

_____

_____

_____

_____

_____

_____

_____

_____

_____

All my answers come to me now
Blessing me with
The way and the how

Thoughts & Notes:

Now that I know
I'm writing the script
I've begun to change
My language a bit

Thoughts & Notes:

I am the block and the doorway
I am the solution I seek
My mind can imprison me
Or set me free

Thoughts & Notes:

Money flows to me easily

AND

I always have more than I need

Thoughts & Notes:

I no longer am
Searching the clouds
Yelling and screaming and
Crying out loud

Responsibility
Is totally mine
And I am no longer
Creating the lie

Thoughts & Notes:

I have the power
The power is in me
I am the architect of my life
And I create the world I see

Thoughts & Notes:

I am my own
Best friend to me
And I determine
My Destiny

Thoughts & Notes:

I am no longer swayed
By others' advices
I'm no longer paying
The guilt-ridden prices
In raising my children
Or quitting my job
I now realize
It's my hand on the knob

Thoughts & Notes:

I rely on myself
And my God-given strength
My faith will sustain me
Until I am quenched

Thoughts & Notes:

I'm opening doors
By instinct alone
Asking others
I will not condone

Although I know not
What's on the other side
My decisions are mine
And I make them with pride

Thoughts & Notes:

The Laws of Prosperity
Are cut and dry
I needn't know how
And I needn't know why
No matter how much I know
Or what I believe
Truth is, the more I give
The more I'll receive

Thoughts & Notes:

"This is a bountiful universe
There is plenty for all of us
I am deserving of this bounty
I am now willing to accept my part of it
I am now receiving all that I desire
The more I receive
The more I can give"

Ananda Abinou

Thoughts & Notes:

"I Am the magic in your wand
Do not doubt I will respond.

I am the Doer of your will
All your needs I will fulfill."

The Universe

Thoughts & Notes:

_____
_____
_____
_____
_____
_____
_____
_____
_____
_____
_____
_____
_____
_____
_____
_____
_____
_____
_____
_____
_____

My mind is the gateway
To all my opportunities
I hold the lock
And I hold the key
I will lock myself in
Or set myself free

Thoughts & Notes:

_____
_____
_____
_____
_____
_____
_____
_____
_____
_____
_____
_____
_____
_____
_____
_____
_____
_____

Since I began to uncover
Myself
And seek the essence which lies
Within
I found some peace, some dignity
I no longer accept
Reality

Thoughts & Notes:

My soul knows the answer
To every question I ask

My soul stands by me
To accomplish any task

Thoughts & Notes:

I keep being my best
And I let God do the rest

Thoughts & Notes:

I am thankful for my health
And all that I can do
I am thankful for my wealth
And all that I accrue

I am thankful for my family
And the love they give to me
I am thankful for the earth
The land and the sea

Thoughts & Notes:

This is a Magical, Mystical
Marvelous, Magnificent Universe

And when we change the Inside,
the Outside
Automatically changes, too!

Thoughts & Notes:

I've come way too far
I won't turn back now
This is my story and
This is my how

To others the pieces
May seem not to fit
But this is my life
And I won't quit!

Thoughts & Notes:

_____
_____
_____
_____
_____
_____
_____
_____
_____
_____
_____
_____
_____
_____
_____
_____
_____

I release any and all
Negative emotions
Toward myself
Or anyone else

Thoughts & Notes:

_____

_____

_____

_____

_____

_____

_____

_____

_____

_____

_____

_____

_____

_____

_____

_____

_____

_____

_____

_____

_____

"I've held you in my loving arms
I've carried you over the hump.

I'm the safety net beneath you
And you're still afraid to jump?"

The Universe

Thoughts & Notes:

I am doing nothing wrong
I am doing everything right

I am learning and I am growing
That is why I'm here
It is the reason for my being

Thoughts & Notes:

Everything is happening in
Divine right-timing
I have no problems
And I am the solution

Thoughts & Notes:

I sit down allowing

My tensions to cease

And come to the place

I call Inner Peace

Thoughts & Notes:

I am receiving my heart's desires
Right now

I am living my dreams
Right now

I am better than I've ever been
Right now

I am living my blessings
Right now

Waiting for nothing
Wanting for nothing

I am receiving everything I desire
Right Now

Thoughts & Notes:

Thank You God
For all that you've done
And all that you do

And God gently whispers:
"I have more for you."

Thoughts & Notes:

_____
_____
_____
_____
_____
_____
_____
_____
_____
_____
_____
_____
_____
_____
_____
_____
_____
_____
_____

The difference between
Alone and Lonely
Is Only
A state of mind

Thoughts & Notes:

_____
_____
_____
_____
_____
_____
_____
_____
_____
_____
_____
_____
_____
_____
_____
_____
_____
_____
_____

There's a time for reaping
There's a time for sowing
And don't ever forget
There's a time for growing

Thoughts & Notes:

_____
_____
_____
_____
_____
_____
_____
_____
_____
_____
_____
_____
_____
_____
_____
_____
_____
_____
_____

Unlike my body
My soul cannot be seen
It's my silent partner
In fulfilling my dreams

Thoughts & Notes:

_____

_____

_____

_____

_____

_____

_____

_____

_____

_____

_____

_____

_____

_____

_____

_____

_____

_____

_____

_____

_____

I'm thankful for this moment
Thankful to be here
To create my life as I see fit
Releasing all my fear

Thoughts & Notes:

The world is but a reflection
Of everything I believe
As I change my thoughts
I change my reality

Thoughts & Notes:

_____

_____

_____

_____

_____

_____

_____

_____

_____

_____

_____

_____

_____

_____

_____

_____

_____

_____

_____

_____

_____

_____

_____

When I'm caught in a problem
And the solution I can't see
I remember these little words
"God's... Got... Me"

I am feeling grateful
For this season of my life
I get stronger and wiser
With every day that goes by

Thoughts & Notes:

_____
_____
_____
_____
_____
_____
_____
_____
_____
_____
_____
_____
_____
_____
_____
_____
_____
_____

My mind can grow
Flowers, vegetables or weeds
But what I put in its soil
My life it will feed

Thoughts & Notes:

_____

_____

_____

_____

_____

_____

_____

_____

_____

_____

_____

_____

_____

_____

_____

_____

_____

_____

_____

I am Spirit in flesh
Come down from above
Spirit in flesh
Manifesting God's Love

Thoughts & Notes:

I am here
To come and to go
To learn and to grow
To shine my light brightly
Wherever I go

Thoughts & Notes:

_____
_____
_____
_____
_____
_____
_____
_____
_____
_____
_____
_____
_____
_____
_____
_____
_____
_____
_____

I'm leaping in faith
And soaring through air
And somehow I know
That God is right there

To lighten the load
To cushion the fall
To lead in the dark
To carry the ball

Thoughts & Notes:

_____
_____
_____
_____
_____
_____
_____
_____
_____
_____
_____
_____
_____
_____
_____
_____
_____
_____

Be oh, so careful
Of the words you speak
For your life will take notice
And begin to seek

Thoughts & Notes:

My success
Is right on the other side ...
Of my fear

Thoughts & Notes:

_____
_____
_____
_____
_____
_____
_____
_____
_____
_____
_____
_____
_____
_____
_____
_____
_____
_____

There's a power in me
But it lives deep down inside

My job is to gain access
To the place where it hides

Thoughts & Notes:

I expect the Universe
To work in my favor
Because when I do ...
It does

Thoughts & Notes:

I am healthy
I am successful
I am everything I want to be

I am wonderful
I am amazing
And my world responds to me

Thoughts & Notes:

_____
_____
_____
_____
_____
_____
_____
_____
_____
_____
_____
_____
_____
_____
_____
_____
_____
_____
_____

Everything happens for a reason
And God always has my back.

Thoughts & Notes:

There's a yearning inside me
Trying to be set free
That message is my soul
It's saying, "I need to be me"

Thoughts & Notes:

To rethink is to restate

To restate is to recreate

Thoughts & Notes:

I know that
All the situations, circumstances,
Resources, contacts, ideas,
Family, friends and money necessary
For the accomplishment of
My Heart's Desires
Are appearing to and for me right now!

Thoughts & Notes:

Your dreams will inspire
Inform and advise you
Just take that first step
And your dreams will take two

Thoughts & Notes:

I will live any reality
I continue to say
Just make sure I'm consistent
Telling myself every day

Thoughts & Notes:

As I wish and I wonder
Contemplate and I ponder
I'm closer than it seems
To achieving my dreams.

Thoughts & Notes:

I believe in me
I acknowledge my own self worth
My confidence is soaring
I am proud of myself

Thoughts & Notes:

It's a very simple process
And it works every time
I place my attention on my goal
And declare "This... is mine."

Thoughts & Notes:

What would you do
If you knew you
Would not ... Could not
Fail

Thoughts & Notes:

Where my attention goes...
My life flows

Thoughts & Notes:

Commitment is the key
That I will use
Commitment is the thing
That will bring me through

Thoughts & Notes:

We get what we ask for
Because we have dominion
Over this space
Our task is to discover
How the asking takes place

Thoughts & Notes:

Everything is happening
Through me and for me
In divine order
And right timing

Thoughts & Notes:

As I go through life
With so many choices it seems

I Remember

Commitment is the answer
To fulfilling my dreams.

Thoughts & Notes:

Success happens when
My mission is bigger than
My insecurities

Thoughts & Notes:

I take time each day
To be at peace
I sit down, relax
And just release

Thoughts & Notes:

Life has no meaning
But the meaning we give it
Our thoughts and beliefs create life
And we live it

Thoughts & Notes:

Me:
"Dear God, please be with me today."

GOD:
*"I Am already and always
with you today and every day."*

Thoughts & Notes:

As surely as I have air to breathe
This is the reality I live and see

I am finally financially free
Money is no longer an issue for me

Thoughts & Notes:

I live my life doing the things I love
Knowing my blessings come from
God, above

And as surely as I
Express the passion in me
God supplies me
With all of my needs

Thoughts & Notes:

Try if you will
Say a little prayer:
God, please take me
Out of despair

Show me the way
Whatever the cost
Show me the way
For I am lost

Thoughts & Notes:

What I think and what I feel
Form my beliefs and will be real
It's all in your attitude
Because what you believe
Will be true for you

Thoughts & Notes:

_____
_____
_____
_____
_____
_____
_____
_____
_____
_____
_____
_____
_____
_____
_____
_____
_____
_____
_____
_____

I am the Author
Of my life
And I am living the stories
I choose to write

Thoughts & Notes:

_____
_____
_____
_____
_____
_____
_____
_____
_____
_____
_____
_____
_____
_____
_____
_____
_____
_____
_____

There is no need for your despair
Your whole life is a living prayer

I am your teacher barring none
I am in the power of your tongue

The Universe

Thoughts & Notes:

I inhale faith
And exhale fear
The outcome I desire
Is, oh, so near

Thoughts & Notes:

Whether getting divorced
Or changing careers
I'm moving my life
Beyond my own fears

Thoughts & Notes:

Holding my focus
Is the key to success
And before I know it
I'm one of the best!

Thoughts & Notes:

I release negative emotions
Frustrations and fears
I sit down, let go
And watch my mind clear

Thoughts & Notes:

_____
_____
_____
_____
_____
_____
_____
_____
_____
_____
_____
_____
_____
_____
_____
_____
_____
_____
_____
_____

Thoughts held deep
Within my mind
They come about
With passing time

Thoughts & Notes:

_____
_____
_____
_____
_____
_____
_____
_____
_____
_____
_____
_____
_____
_____
_____
_____
_____
_____
_____
_____
_____
_____

Today is the day
I wash away all my fears
Today is the day
I dry up all my tears

Thoughts & Notes:

Just like when I eat
I use a fork and knife
Commitment is my tool
For this journey called Life

Thoughts & Notes:

_____

_____

_____

_____

_____

_____

_____

_____

_____

_____

_____

_____

_____

_____

_____

_____

_____

_____

_____

_____

Very few people
Are living their dreams
But the fact that we're here
Means we can
Wouldn't it seem?

Thoughts & Notes:

My desires are manifesting

As sure as I stand

I can manifest anything

With a wave of my hand

Thoughts & Notes:

"Your questions I respond to
Your needs I do provide.

How else can I assure you
I'm right here, by your side."

The Universe

Thoughts & Notes:

I will wait no longer
To create my story
I will be who I came here to be
And walk in my glory

Thoughts & Notes:

I can attract

Anything I desire

I don't have to work a job

That I don't like and retire

Thoughts & Notes:

_____
_____
_____
_____
_____
_____
_____
_____
_____
_____
_____
_____
_____
_____
_____
_____
_____
_____
_____
_____

I stand for the truth
Within my soul, and
I ignore the reality
No matter what I'm told

Thoughts & Notes:

I create my reality
Through the thoughts that I speak
I am made in God's image
I am strong, not weak

Thoughts & Notes:

It's a stress-filled world
But we can live stress free
All we've got to do
Is let go and just be

Thoughts & Notes:

What brings you joy
Like nothing else can
Puts a smile on your face
Can put money in your hand?

This is your passion
Let it rise to the surface
Celebrate your life
And begin living in your purpose!

Thoughts & Notes:

I forgive and let go
For we reap
What we sow

Thoughts & Notes:

_____
_____
_____
_____
_____
_____
_____
_____
_____
_____
_____
_____
_____
_____
_____
_____
_____
_____
_____

Walk by faith
As you do what you do
Knowing that the Universe
Has always got you

Thoughts & Notes:

Think about the life you're living
And what you want it to be
Write it down, believe in it
And just you wait and see

The day will come
When you'll be shocked
For as you look around
Everywhere you turn you'll see
The thing that you wrote down!

Thoughts & Notes:

_____
_____
_____
_____
_____
_____
_____
_____
_____
_____
_____
_____
_____
_____
_____
_____
_____
_____
_____

Seek and ye shall find
It does not matter you are blind

You will have what you desire
When you summon me with fire!

The Universe

Thoughts & Notes:

Our God-given gifts
Are all that we need
We are the flowers
And they are the seeds

Thoughts & Notes:

Nothing becomes anything

Until my mind labels it

Something

Thoughts & Notes:

_____
_____
_____
_____
_____
_____
_____
_____
_____
_____
_____
_____
_____
_____
_____
_____
_____
_____
_____
_____
_____

Thank You, God, for blessing me

With life's most precious necessity

For as you've given

Air to breathe

I know you'll satisfy

My needs

Thoughts & Notes:

_____

_____

_____

_____

_____

_____

_____

_____

_____

_____

_____

_____

_____

_____

_____

_____

_____

_____

_____

_____

_____

My Success

Is But One Thought Away

Thoughts & Notes:

I always remember

It's not if I can or I can't

It's if I will or I won't

Thoughts & Notes:

I manifest my life

Without fear or hesitation

Because I believe in myself

And conscious creation

Thoughts & Notes:

Consistent, Continuous
Constant Commitment

I've got it, and
That's all it takes!

Thoughts & Notes:

_____
_____
_____
_____
_____
_____
_____
_____
_____
_____
_____
_____
_____
_____
_____
_____
_____
_____
_____
_____
_____
_____

Who needs a wand

When I can wave my hand

Turn the world around

Right from where I stand

Thoughts & Notes:

_____

_____

_____

_____

_____

_____

_____

_____

_____

_____

_____

_____

_____

_____

_____

_____

_____

_____

_____

_____

As I open

Each new door

I know I am

Provided for

Thoughts & Notes:

I AM.

Not the Mind.

Thoughts & Notes:

I let go of my fears

My strength is inside

The truth of my being

I will no longer hide

Thoughts & Notes:

I am so grateful the Universe

Is always working for my highest good

And things are all ways

Working out as they should

Thoughts & Notes:

_____
_____
_____
_____
_____
_____
_____
_____
_____
_____
_____
_____
_____
_____
_____
_____
_____
_____
_____

I am allowing Divine guidance

To enter my life

To alleviate the struggles and

Eliminate the strife

Thoughts & Notes:

No longer must I
Or will I depend

Upon a mate
Or any other friend

I have the power
I have the strength

To mold my life
And shape my world

Thoughts & Notes:

Miracles are here
Miracles are there

Upon my command
Miracles are everywhere

Thoughts & Notes:

"It is me you are not seeing
I'm in the fiber of your being

Just take one step
And I'll take two

All I'm trying to tell you is
I've got you."

The Universe

Thoughts & Notes:

_____

_____

_____

_____

_____

_____

_____

_____

_____

_____

_____

_____

_____

_____

_____

_____

_____

_____

_____

_____

_____

I am trusting the process
To unfold naturally

I am never alone
God is always with me

Thoughts & Notes:

I am Awakening and

Illuminating day by day

Creating my desires

Using the words that I say

Thoughts & Notes:

_____
_____
_____
_____
_____
_____
_____
_____
_____
_____
_____
_____
_____
_____
_____
_____
_____
_____
_____
_____

I am learning and I am growing

I am listening to my inner knowing

Thoughts & Notes:

_____
_____
_____
_____
_____
_____
_____
_____
_____
_____
_____
_____
_____
_____
_____
_____
_____
_____
_____

I am the change in my world

That I wish to see

Because I understand the change

All begins with me

Thoughts & Notes:

I'm living my life
Claiming what I need
Knowing what I claim
Comes easily to me

Thoughts & Notes:

Be in your life

Doing what you do

Knowing what you want

Is coming effortlessly to you

Thoughts & Notes:

I shine my light

As a beacon in the night

Showing the way for others

To shine their lights bright

Thoughts & Notes:

_____
_____
_____
_____
_____
_____
_____
_____
_____
_____
_____
_____
_____
_____
_____
_____
_____
_____

"Ask of Me," I'm crying out.
"Your word is my command!"
"Don't you know I'm here for you?
Why can't you understand?"

The Universe

Thoughts & Notes:

_____
_____
_____
_____
_____
_____
_____
_____
_____
_____
_____
_____
_____
_____
_____
_____
_____
_____
_____

My miracle is coming

I can see it in my sites

It's coming 'round the bend

And the timing is just right

Thoughts & Notes:

_____
_____
_____
_____
_____
_____
_____
_____
_____
_____
_____
_____
_____
_____
_____
_____
_____
_____
_____
_____
_____
_____

As Earth welcomes the sunlight

Into its pores

I welcome Prosperity

In through my doors

Thoughts & Notes:

Receiving More
Lives in the death
Of wanting more
Yet, accepting less

Thoughts & Notes:

_____
_____
_____
_____
_____
_____
_____
_____
_____
_____
_____
_____
_____
_____
_____
_____
_____
_____
_____
_____

I am now living my life in alignment

With who I came here to be

And what I came here to Learn

Teach, Express and See

Thoughts & Notes:

"What's happened to your faith?
Could it be easier said than done?
My child,
There's nothing that's impossible
For you and I are One."

The Universe

Printed in Great Britain
by Amazon